GEOMETRIC PATTERNS & BORDERS

GEOMETRIC PATTERNS
& BORDERS

David Wade

VNR **VAN NOSTRAND REINHOLD COMPANY**
New York   Cincinnati   Toronto   London   Melbourne

Copyright © 1982 by David Wade

Library of Congress Catalog Card Number 81-23152

ISBN 0-442-29240-6 (cloth)
    0-442-29241-4 (paper)

Printed in the United States of America

Published in U.K. by Wildwood House Ltd.

Published simultaneously in U.S.A. in 1982
by Van Nostrand Reinhold Company Inc.
135 West 50th Street
New York, NY 10020

Van Nostrand Reinhold Publishing
1410 Birchmount Road
Scarborough, Ontario M1P 2E7, Canada

16 15 14 13 12 11 10 9 8 7 6 5 4 3 2 1

Library of Congress Cataloging in Publication Data
Wade, David
    Geometric patterns & borders.

    1. Repetitive patterns (Decorative arts)
2. Geometrical drawing.   3. Borders, Ornamental
(Decorative arts)   I. Title.   II. Title: Geometric
patterns and borders.
NK1570.W28   1982   745.4   81-23152
                                      AACR2
ISBN 0-442-29241-4 (pbk.)

The patterns reproduced in this book may be used
or copied without reference to the publisher.

Contents

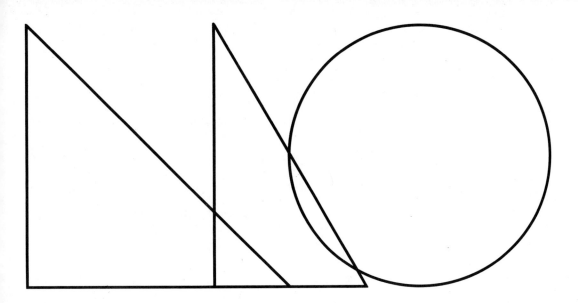

Preface

You may be sure that any decoration is futile . . . when it does not remind you of something beyond itself. – William Morris

Pattern and symmetry so thoroughly permeate the fabric of our universe that it is hardly surprising that they should be prominent in any understanding or description of it. This is why patterns are "discovered" by scientists and "created" by artists. In science a familiarity with the laws of symmetry underpins atomic physics, crystallography, chemistry and much else; in the realm of art there has probably never been a culture that has not used pattern.

The impulse to decorate in a specifically geometric mode seems to be fairly universal and because it involves measurement and planning always carries with it some sense of underlying reasoning or logic, even as the product of "primitive" cultures. Pattern often derives directly from the constraints imposed by the medium, as in basket-weaving or brickwork, but geometric forms have an attraction of their own for their own sake. That some cultures have a definite inclination toward these forms is evident from their frequent mention in this book for providing source material. The prime example is, of course, the Islamic peoples, whose preoccupation with geometric ornament of all kinds is well known. In the European tradition, by contrast, pattern in general has suffered a consistent downgrading since the medieval period and has been relegated to a comparatively minor role. The reaction against this trend is evident in the general reevaluation that art has undergone in recent times and, in fact, traces back to the movement in which Owen Jones and William Morris played leading roles.

It is beyond the scope of this book to delve into the subtle reasons behind such various cultural responses, but it is clear that patterns can carry a distinct sense of cultural identity as demonstrated by the "step" patterns of Central and South America, and the convoluted "key" patterns of the Celts. Similarly Islamic geometric patterns are marked by their inclination to a-centricity.

The firm, soundly based Chinese examples seem to tell of a confident and enduring civilization. Japanese patterns though similar seem, by contrast, to achieve a sharper, prettier quality, and so on.

A cultural identity may, in fact, cling to the simplest of patterns. On the other hand some configurations seem to have an almost universal significance. All this may be of little interest to that still current tendency in art which rejects tradition and discipline of any kind, though in response to this one might say that creative freedom is in direct proportion to the knowledge of what is possible. In presenting this collection of patterns from sources widely separated in space and time, together with indications as to their construction, it is hoped to add to the sum of creative possibilities.

Introduction

The notion of pattern derives from the recognition of a periodic recurrence; that is to say, two elements are required: a repeat motif conjoined with a structured or rhythmic base. In mathematical terms this constitutes an *ordered array* and thereby establishes pattern as a branch of symmetry. Other classes under this latter heading include bilateral symmetry, of which the Rorschach blot is an example, and solid or three-dimensional symmetry. Two-dimensional patterns express symmetry in three distinct ways, *planar*, *linear* and *centered*. The *planar* group is comprised of the infinite patterns, which may extend in any direction to completely fill the plane. These consist of a repeated motif laid out regularly on a grid or net, the simplest example being the net itself. In the *linear* group the repeat extends along a line to produce a frieze or border. *Centered* patterns are generally finite and constructed around a point, as in the rose windows of cathedrals. This book concerns itself with the first two (and the most useful) of these categories, the infinite pattern and the border.*

figs.1-3

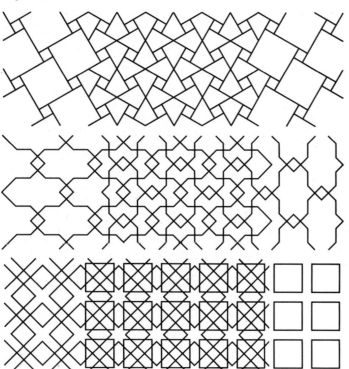

In the field of design and ornamentation all pattern is "geometric" to the extent that the term implies structural formality. The patterns presented here are, however, geometric in a narrower sense, in that they use only straight lines and circles (or arcs), most often based on a simple square or triangular grid. My aim in compiling this collection is to present examples that might be both useful in themselves as design source material and serve to demonstrate methods of pattern construction in a more general way. For this reason I have adopted a stripped-down, graphic presentation that, together with an indication of the underlying grids, serves, I hope, to emphasize the structural basis of the patterns. In adopting this style of presentation I have concentrated on the essential design and disregarded the actual medium of the originals, which are as various as may be imagined. Presenting the designs in this undiluted way carries the advantage of avoiding any preconception. For instance, the design in fig. 59 is taken from a Peruvian canoe oar, but might as easily be applied to, say, a furnishing fabric. The elements of pattern given here are the bare bones and may be fleshed out and embellished as required.

Another advantage of this unadorned form of presentation is that it enables the similarities and relationships between different patterns to be seen more clearly. Cross references of this sort are indicated in the book as (ref.-), and originals of which the example given is a variation are indicated as (var.-). It may be found also that the same pattern can be viewed in quite different ways, as assembled components for instance, or as interwoven profiles or overlaid figures. It is this "pattern consciousness", the awareness of the interplay of figures on a grid, that is at the heart of creative pattern design. The overlay, as well as being a way of viewing and analysing many patterns is, of course, an effective device in pattern construction. In the three examples given in figs. I-3, the first shows a simple arrangement of squares brought together with its mirror image in a 45° rotation, the second consists of a "mouj" pattern laid on itself at 90° and the third example blends two simple square patterns at 45°. All of these combinations produce patterns that are greater than the sum of their parts.

As far as possible, within the limits of the style adopted for this book, the patterns are presented as found at source. It will be noticed that these fall into four main categories, namely, line, solid, lattice, and interlace. Four versions of what is essentially the same "star and cross" pattern in figs. i–iv show how these different forms may translate any one to another. Taking the line drawing, fig. i, this is easily transformed, by blocking in, to the solid version, fig. ii. Thickening out this original line leads to a lattice, fig. iii, and an interlace is achieved by weaving this new, thickened line alternately over and under, fig. iv.

Arcs and circles are used in the analyses to denote equivalence, and small arrows indicate critical intersections. Angles other than 90°, 60°, 45°, or 30° are generally indicated. The patterns, other than the most elementary, are credited with a source. Since many patterns have a wide currency, this derivation is only indicative and should not necessarily be taken to imply exclusivity.

*There are no less than seventeen forms of symmetry in the *planar* group, seven in the *linear*. A most comprehensive and intelligible survey of these may be found in *Geometric Symmetry* by Lockwood and Macmillan, Cambridge University Press, 1978.

Figs. I–IV

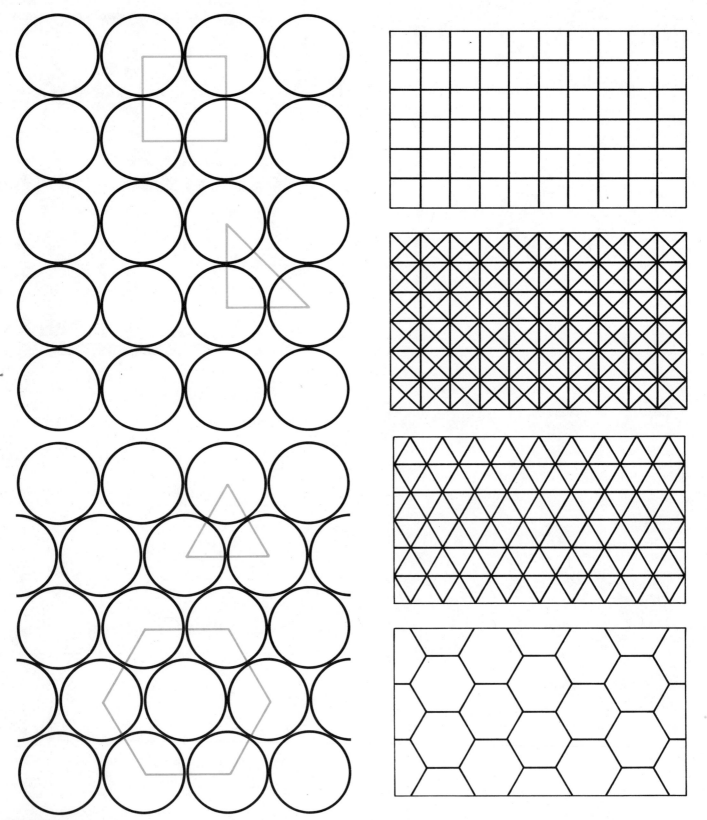

Figs. V–X

The Basic Grids

Given that the term "pattern" implies a formal arrangement of a repeated element, the essential preliminary in pattern construction is to establish the supporting framework. This necessitates the "division of the plane". It is a curious fact that a complete equipartition of a flat surface (the Euclidean Plane) can only be effected by those regular polygons whose internal angles are 60°, 90°, and 120°: the square, the equilateral triangle, and the hexagon. The nets or grids thus produced may further be traced back to two distinct forms of circles in contact with axial alignments of 90° and 60° respectively, figs. v, vi. Since the hexagon itself may further be constructed on a triangular grid, the triangular and the square grid are sufficient as the underlying structure of the majority of the patterns shown in this book. The usefulness of these two basic grids is increased by doubling the number of gridlines. This produces, in the case of the square, a new grid, fig. viii, with lines at 45°, and a triangular equivalent with lines at 30°, see figs. 278–279. (It is of more than passing interest that these nets are made up of the two "basic triangles" of Plato which were for him and his followers the basis of all matter, and the point of contact between the world of ideas and the material world. These two right-angled triangles are also familiar as the standard set squares of studio and drawing office.)

As well as the three regular grids and the derivatives described above, a series of semi- and demi-regular equipartitions, 22 in all, may be of interest to designers. These, too, may be seen as deriving from circles in contact, and as in the case of the regular grids, the centers of the circles form the nodes of the tessellations. The complete range of these may be found in the Appendix.

The significance of the grids so far described goes beyond purely visual considerations, but there are, of course, many other plane-filling systems of particular interest to designers. To begin with, all the grids mentioned above are absolutely deformable: nets may be formed of like rectangles, rhomboids and scalene triangles, offering limitless design potential. The price exacted for this wealth of possibilities is, however, correspondingly high – the sacrifice of degrees and types of symmetry. It is worth noting though, from the point of view of design variation, that any pattern based on a grid will, naturally, conform to a desired obliquity.

Other groups of plane-filling figures are worth mentioning in a design context. These include pairs of squares in any ratio, an arrangement that will utilize tiles of any two given sizes, fig. xi. This pattern, like any other grid-based pattern, is readily deformable, in this case to pairs of rhombs, fig. xii. Also in this family are arrangements of squares and rectangles, with infinite possible variations in their relative sizes, fig. xiii. Another characteristic group is that which consists of rectangles of the same or unequal length laid at 90° angles to each other (figs. xiv and xv respectively). These latter, familiar as parquet blocks in flooring, derive from rectangles made up of squares. The formation as a whole, therefore, is founded on a square grid.

A special case, having an affinity with all these, occurs on the triangular grid, where hexagons and equilateral triangles in an infinitely variable series will fill the plane (figs. xvi and xvii). The mid-point, where the sides of each polygon are equal, is reached at the semi-regular tessellation shown in fig. 2 in the Appendix.

The point of particularizing these various grids, nets or tessellations (the terms are virtually interchangeable in this context), is to set out the possibilities and constraints inherent in pattern construction, because, of course, these apply whether one is conscious of them or not and whether one is working within a guiding tradition or without.

Figs. XI–XVII

Coloring Schemes

In the matter of coloring it is a fair generalization to say that square-based patterns require an absolute minimum of two colors whereas those based on a triangular grid generally require a minimum of three, although there are exceptions to this. The possibilities and limitations here are most clearly demonstrated in the series of Counterchange patterns, the simplest example of which is the checker of a chess board. The pattern in fig. 4 is an elementary example that employs a two color (or tone) scheme. Fig. 5 shows a counterchange drawn from a triangular grid, but based essentially on just two of the three reticulations, and expressable thereby in a two-color scheme. Visually, however, patterns derived from the triangular grid require a minimum of three colors or tones, as in fig. 6. This Egyptian example, typical of many from the section on Islamic patterns, may be expressed in three colors; others need four and most accept a six-color rendition.

Curiously the square grid itself can support a three-color scheme as in fig. 7. A "doubling up" of this arrangement establishes the possibility that the square grid will also support a six-color system. A variation of this easily produces a five-colorway scheme, and naturally the checker pattern itself extends to a four-color version. These terms apply to all of the square-based counterchange patterns including those rotated through 90°, also to many of the interlock and ecalé patterns. Most of this latter group may be expressed as simple counterchange patterns, but as a cautionary example fig. 8, though square-based, requires a three-color treatment.

Stratiform or layered patterns offer less color constraints. When the strata consists of a single, interlocking profile, as in fig. 9, the color series is infinitely variable. In the more complex varieties using two or more different interlocking layers the repeating series should be a multiple of these (see figs. 10 and 391–394).

figs. 4–6

figs. 7 & 8

fig.9

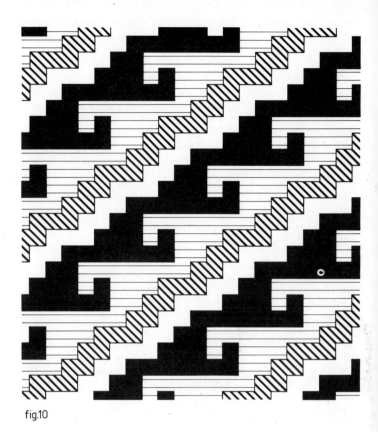

fig.10

Notes on the Patterns

The general progression of the patterns presented here moves from the simple towards greater complexity, in terms of the underlying geometry. The sequence adopted for the infinite patterns is roughly followed in the section devoted to Borders.

Square-based patterns then are the natural starting point being, by virtue of their simplicity, the most universal and useful form (figs. 11–75). These can often be made more interesting by the simple expedient of rotation through 45° (see figs. 51, 52, 54, 55). The addition of the **Diagonal** to square-based patterns considerably enlarges the design scope, bringing in the option of an alternate series of "pathways". This doubling of the basic net (fig. viii), consists, in fact, of two square grids in overlay bearing a proportional relationship of √2:1 (figs. 76–153). The diagonal taken across two or more squares together offers interesting possibilities too. This technique, favoured by Celtic illuminators, seems, for some reason, to be little used or undiscovered elsewhere, but is a useful device in pattern building (figs. 154–170).

The **Counterchange**, may be defined as "a series of figures, identical in form, which interlock, but contrast alternately". These have already been referred to in the notes on coloring schemes. Various examples may be found in this book as solid versions of elementary square-based patterns (see figs. 24–32 and 41–48). A special and interesting group of counterchange patterns are those shown in figs. 188–203. These are a series of identical

figures that interlock when rotated through 90°. Since these are essentially square-based they may be, and usually are, expressed in a minimum of two colors or contrasting tones. Figs. 171–177 show patterns made up of squares in various special arrangements. These are of particular use in creating more complex patterns from a basic square unit, such as a tile. This sort of assemblage of regular figures lends itself well to patchwork too, as do many of the examples given in the Appendix.

The **Swastika**, **Interlock**, **Key**, **Knot** and **Spiral** are loose definitions for types of pattern that seem to have an almost universal popularity. The examples given are predominantly square-based, but with a few triangular-based varieties.

The three conventional modes of **Weave** demonstrate yet again the constraints and possibilities in Geometry that are so much the subject of this book (figs. 240–242). The two principle categories of square and triangular are represented here, the square occurring in its regular form as the commonplace warp and weft of most woven materials. The triangular, however, is found in semi-regular form (see fig. 2 in the Appendix), preferred to avoid the "piling" at the nodes or intersections that would occur with the regular form. The third, and in practical terms last, conventional woven form is that shown at fig. 242. This gives a denser, more integrated weave than the previous two, and for this reason is familiar from its use in cane-plaited seating in furniture. This **weave** is also interesting because it reveals a grid that leads directly to the "Star and Cross" pattern (see below). Following these three are a group of designs obviously inspired by and imitating woven patterns, though some of these cannot be used three-dimensionally.

Patterns based on the **Triangular Grid** convey a dynamism lacking in the square, but do not enjoy anything like the same ubiquity. Familiar as the patterns emanating from this grid are in the Islamic world and Central and Eastern Asia, it is perhaps surprising that these have never found widespread acceptance in the West. The particular fascination with the potential of this net for the Muslim *ornemaniste* is evident from the series shown in figs. 296–323. This collection of quite easily constructed patterns also testifies to the sheer variety of forms that can be extracted from such an elementary base. The examples given are from a wide range of originals including textiles, miniature paintings, stucco and ceramics.

The Hexagon is, of course, one of the three regular figures that will completely fill the plane and may itself be constructed on a triangular grid. These properties seem to endow the hexagon with great design potential; many patterns emerge just from overlays of hexagons of different sizes. Naturally patterns from overlaid hexagons, and others involving hexagons will all be drawn up on the triangular grid (figs. 324–347). The prime example in nature of a regular lattice structure is the familiar hexagonal **Comb-cell** of the honey bee. It is this that seems to have inspired a family of patterns that are widely popular in China and Japan (figs. 348–350). In common with the arrangements of squares and the various semi-regular tessellations, these designs, because of the basic simplicity of their components, seem particularly relevant to patchwork and the like.

Similar to the hexagon, though rather less adaptable, the **Octagon** will generate patterns through overlaps. This figure alone will not fill the plane. To do so a secondary component is required – the square. This arrangement is another of those falling into the category of semi-regular tessellations (fig. 6 Appendix). The octagon enjoys a fairly wide distribution and is the highest order of polygon (figs. 351–373). Interestingly the 5-, 7-, 9-, 10- and 11-gons are rarely used in patterns, because of the geometrical difficulties of incorporating these into a plane-filling scheme.* The final polygon to be considered here is the **Dodecagon** or twelve-sided plane figure. This has some interest as an element of pattern and features quite prominently in the groups of semi- and demi-regular tessellations (see Appendix). Requiring an equilateral triangle as a necessary complement to fill the plane, this figure has, by virtue of the divisors of its number of sides (3 by 4), an affinity with both the square and triangular grids.

I have adopted the term **Stratiform** to apply to those patterns structured in layers that extend laterally (figs. 381–394). The strata may consist of a single interlocking band or of a repeating series. In the latter cases the component elements are usually differentiated by coloring or toning (dealt with in the section on coloring schemes). Simple examples of this type of patterning often derive quite naturally from weaving techniques and are frequently found in the woven artifacts of quite primitive cultures. The example shown in fig. 383 is from African basketwork, though this sort of formation is also familiar from heavy textile weaves.

The **Star and Cross** pattern may be laid out on a square net, but the essential grid on which it is based is shown in the woven pattern in fig. 242. This pattern derives from a maintenance of the square through rotation: the "star" component consists of two squares set at 45°; the "cross" element is the necessary complement to fill the plane. Although examples of this arrangement can be found anywhere from Spain to Japan, this is another of those patterns that, for some reason, is not part of the design repertoire of the modern West. On its own this profile gives a delightful tile shape, and it also provides the basis for many variations (figs. 416–435).

Another unfamiliar form is that of the **Mouj**. This is an Iranian term for a pattern component that is, essentially, an irregular dodecagon. Like the star and cross formation, patterns using this figure are found in most Muslim countries.

The significance of the various arrangements of circles in contact has been shown in figs. v–x, and mention has been made of the fact that these can be seen to underlie not only the three regular grids, but also all of the semi- and demi-regular tessellations. Figs. 433–448 show some of the common **Arrangements of Overlaid Circles**, interesting in themselves, and for their pattern-generating qualities. Some of the patterns emanating from these arrangements are to be found in figs. 449–473, the section devoted to **Patterns Using Circles and Arcs**.

Ecalé or fishscale patterns constitute an interesting and widely used group, well known in the Classical world. The three most common varieties are shown (figs. 474–476), and two interesting Chinese variations are given (figs. 477 and 478).

The series of designs from **Borneo** are included as a group because of their fresh, distinctive quality. The rich fund of patterns from this source are a good example of a highly evolved sense of graphic composition issuing from an otherwise "primitive" culture.

The **Petal** patterns, interesting in themselves, also reveal a useful device for pattern building. This is the expansion of one component in a given pattern to the point of overlap, and the subsequent diminution of other parts. In this way fig. 483 goes to make fig. 484, and in a similar way fig. 485 becomes 486. The last in this group, fig. 487, enjoys a wide distribution in the Islam almost attaining the status of a "classic" pattern.

Many of the categories described above have an equivalent in the section on **Borders**, and the general sequence in this section echoes that of the infinite patterns, so that there are square-based, triangular-based, "star and cross" borders using circles etc. The border is the natural, containing, complement to the infinite pattern. The examples given are intended to be useful both directly, as source material, and also as a guide to border construction in a more general way.

*In the pattern-crazed periods in the history of Islam, these very difficulties were taken as a challenge, but these rarefied examples are beyond the scope of the present work.

Appendix

The eight semi-regular grids figs. 1–8
The fourteen demi-regular grids figs. 9–22

These computer-generated drawings of the complete range of semi- and demi-regular grids are reproduced, with permission, from *An Atlas for Designers* by Geoff Edwards, printed by the Middlesex Polytechnic. Apart from the three regular grids, these demonstrate all the possible variations in plane-filling using regular polygons only.

11 JAPAN

12 JAPAN

13 CELTIC

14 JAPAN

15

16

17

18

19

20

21

22

23

24

25

26

27

28

29

30

31

32

33

34

35

36

37

38

39

40

41

42

43

44

45

46

47

48

49 SPAIN

50 SPAIN

51 SPAIN

52 SPAIN

53 SPAIN

54 CONGO

55 GREECE

57 SPAIN

58 CHINA

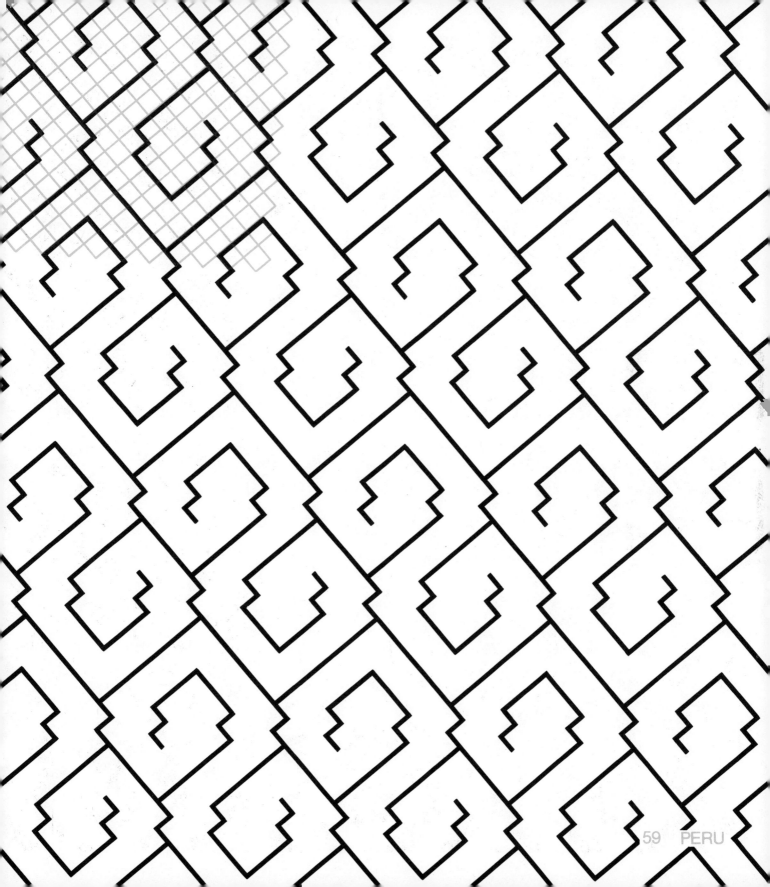

60 TURKEY

61 SPAIN

62 SPAIN

63 SPAIN

64 SPAIN

65 CHINA

66 CHINA

67 CHINA

68 ETHIOPIA

69 CONGO

75 SPAIN

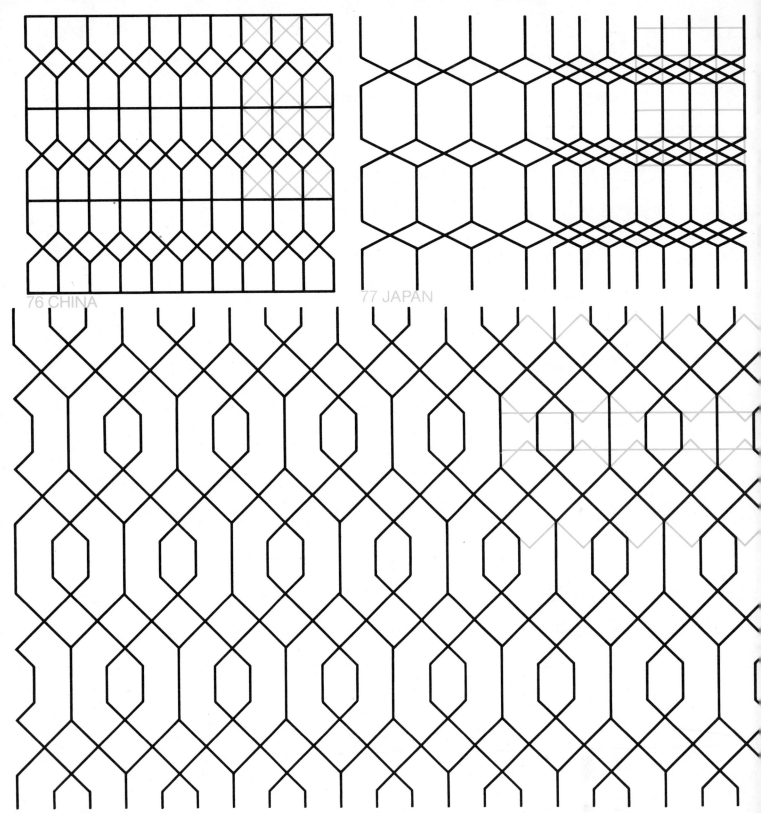

76 CHINA

77 JAPAN

78 JAPAN

79

80

81 TURKEY

82 GOTHIC

83 GOTHIC

84 GOTHIC

← 85 SPAIN

86 MOROCCO

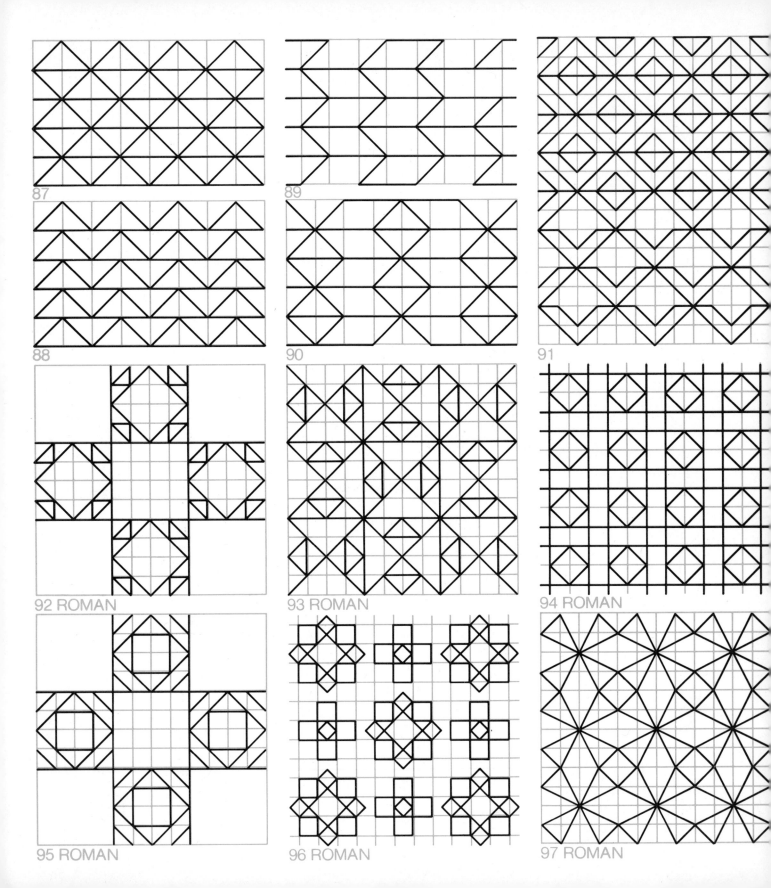

87

89

88

90

91

92 ROMAN

93 ROMAN

94 ROMAN

95 ROMAN

96 ROMAN

97 ROMAN

98

100

99

101

102

103

104

105

106

107

108

109 CHINA

110 CELTIC

111 CELTIC

112 CELTIC

113

114

115

116

117 ITALY

118 ITALY

119 CHINA

120 FRANCE

121 CELTIC

↓ 123 CHINA   122 ITALY

↑ 126 IRAN   ↓ 127 CHINA

128 CELTIC

129 CELTIC

130 CELTIC

131 CELTIC

132 CELTIC

133 CELTIC

134 CELTIC

135 CELTIC

136 CELTIC

137 CELTIC

138 MOROCCO

139 SPAIN

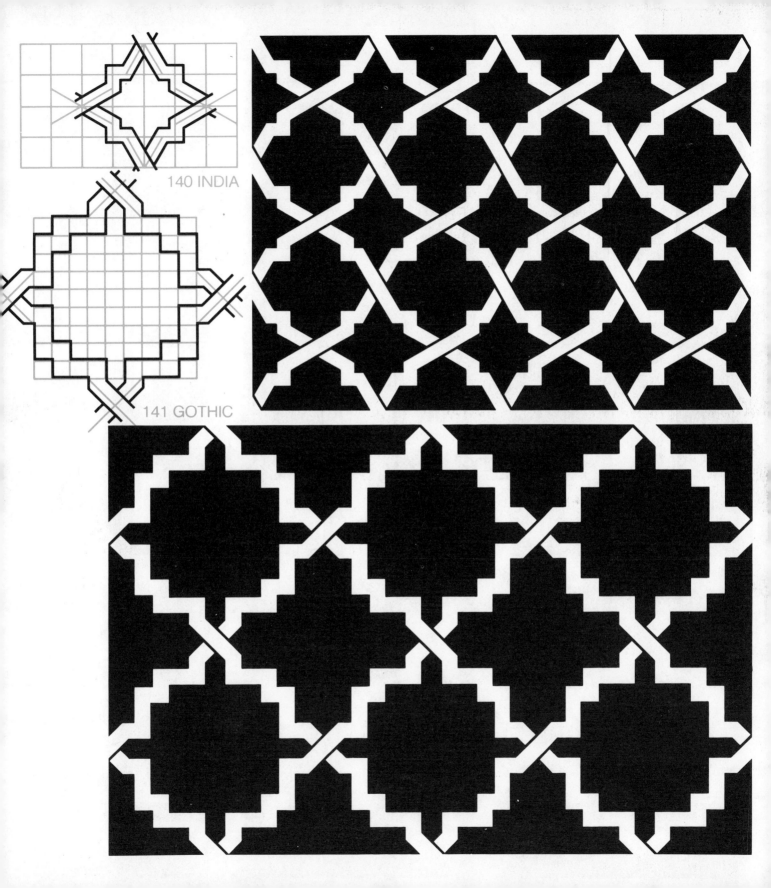

140 INDIA

141 GOTHIC

142 MEXICO

143
CHILE

144 PERU

146 ZAIRE

47 CELEBES

150 EGYPT

151 EGYPT

152 IRAN

153 IRAN

154 CELTIC

155 CELTIC

156 CELTIC

157 CELTIC

158 CELTIC

159 CELTIC

160 CELTIC

161 CELTIC

162 CELTIC

163 CELTIC

164

165

166

167

168

169

170

171

172 (ref. 376)

173

174 (ref. 375)

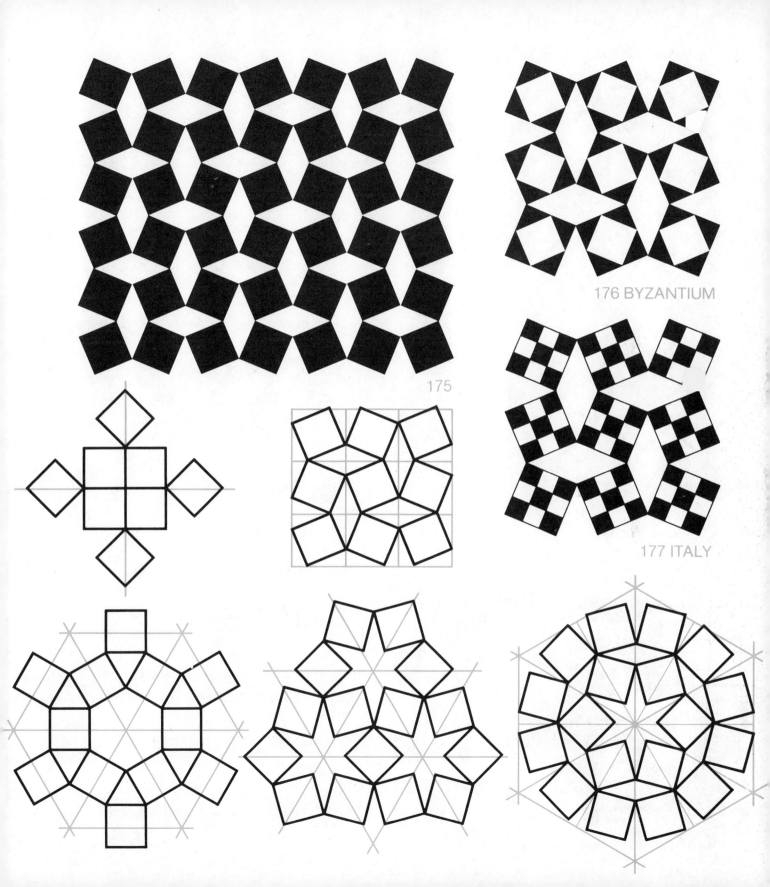

175

176 BYZANTIUM

177 ITALY

178 CHINA

179 JAPAN

180 CELTIC

181 IRAQ

182 CELTIC

183 CELTIC

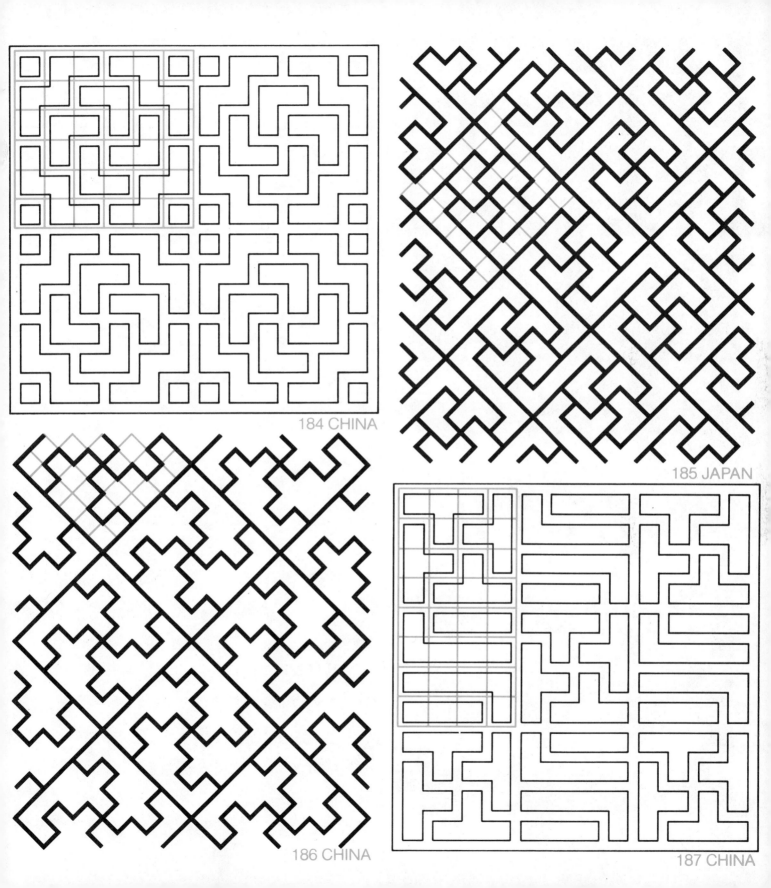

184 CHINA

185 JAPAN

186 CHINA

187 CHINA

188

189

190 BYZANTIUM (var. 188, 189)

191

192 TURKEY (var. 191)

193

194

195

196 CHINA (var. 191, 195)

197 IRAN

198 SPAIN

199 INDIA

200 EGYPT

202

203

204

205

206 AFGHANISTAN

207 AFGHANISTAN

208 AFGHANISTAN

209 AFGHANISTAN

211 JAPAN

212 JAPAN

213 VENEZUELA

214 INDONESIA

215 JAPAN

216 CHINA

217 IRAN, CHINA, JAPAN

218 CHINA

219 JAPAN

220 MONGOLIA

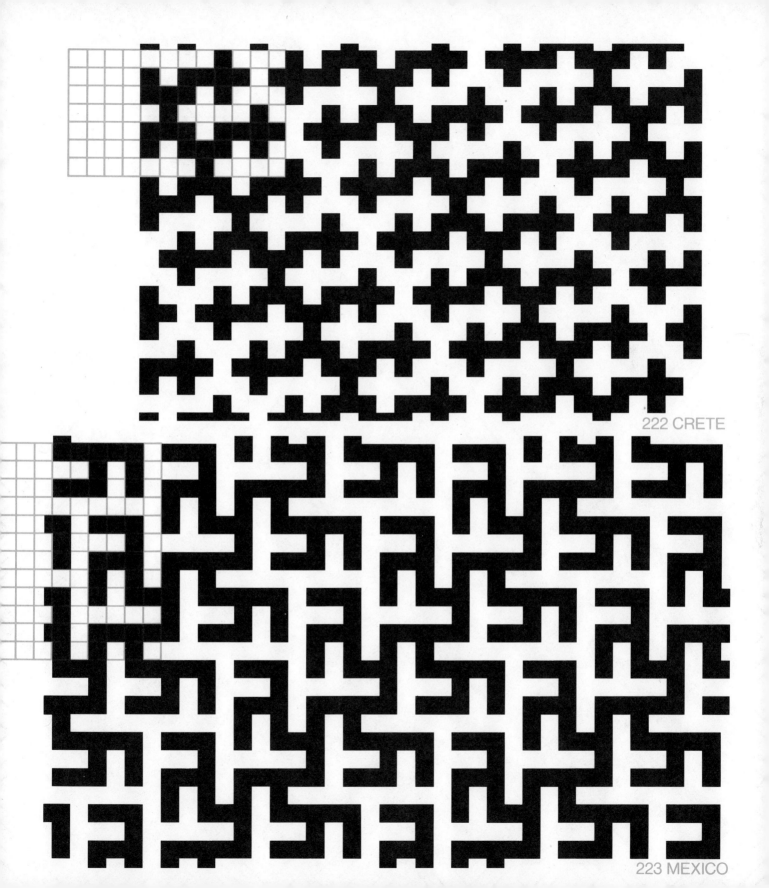

222 CRETE

223 MEXICO

224 CELTIC

225 CELEBES

226 GREECE

227 PERU

228 TURKEY

229 ENGLAND

230 CHINA

231 GOTHIC

↓ 232 CELTIC

233 CHINA

234 JAPAN

235 CHINA

236 JAPAN

237 JAPAN

240

241

242

243

244

245 GOTHIC

246 JAPAN

250

251

252

253

254

255

256

257

258

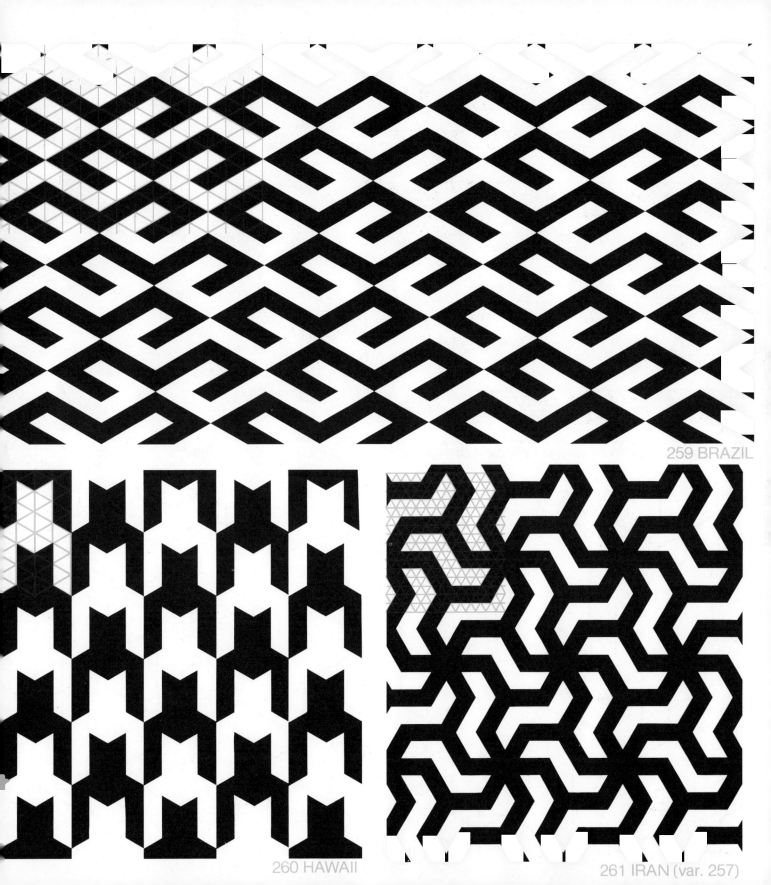

259 BRAZIL

260 HAWAII

261 IRAN (var. 257)

262 IRAQ

263 MOROCCO

264 IRAN

265 JAPAN

266 CHINA

267 JAPAN

268 JAPAN

269 JAPAN

270 WIDESPREAD ISLAMIC (ref. 324)

271 JAPAN

272 JAPAN

273 JAPAN

274 JAPAN

275 JAPAN

276 CELTIC (ref. 134-137)

277 ECUADOR

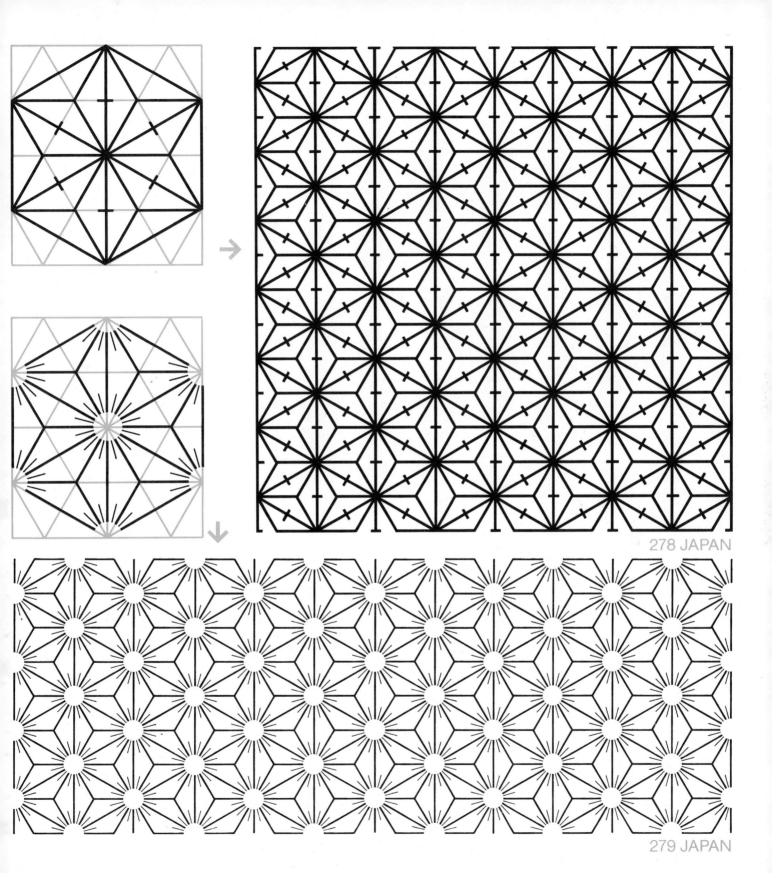

278 JAPAN

279 JAPAN

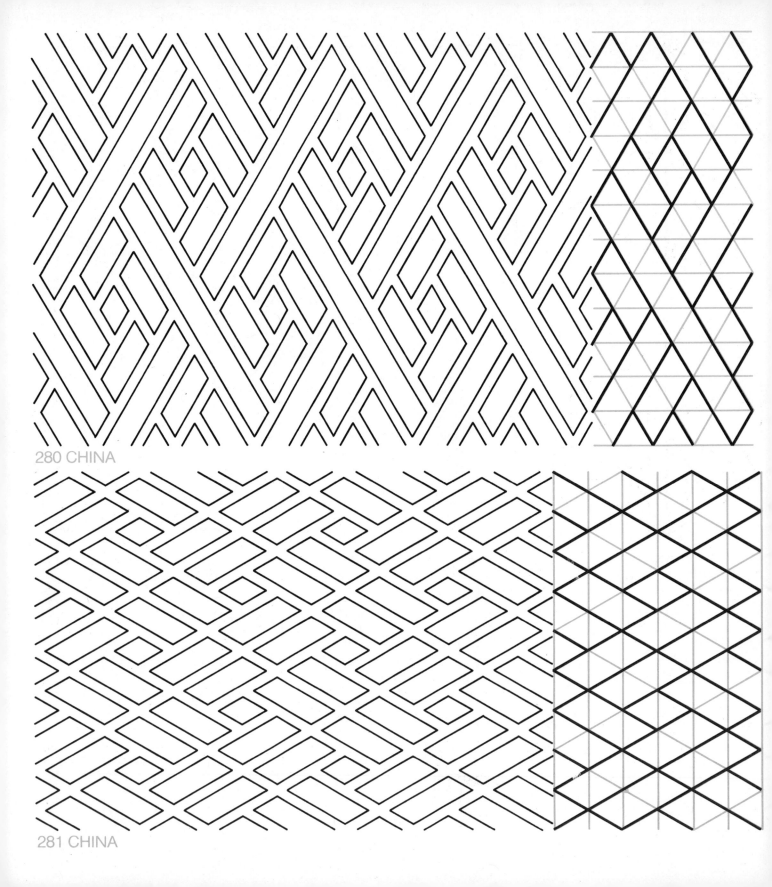

280 CHINA

281 CHINA

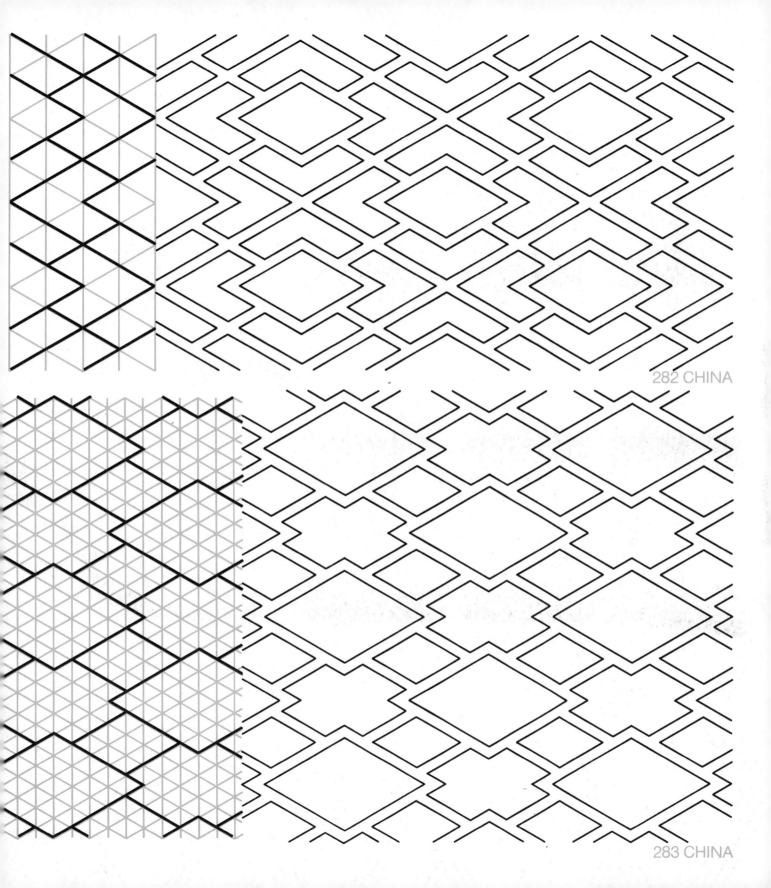

282 CHINA

283 CHINA

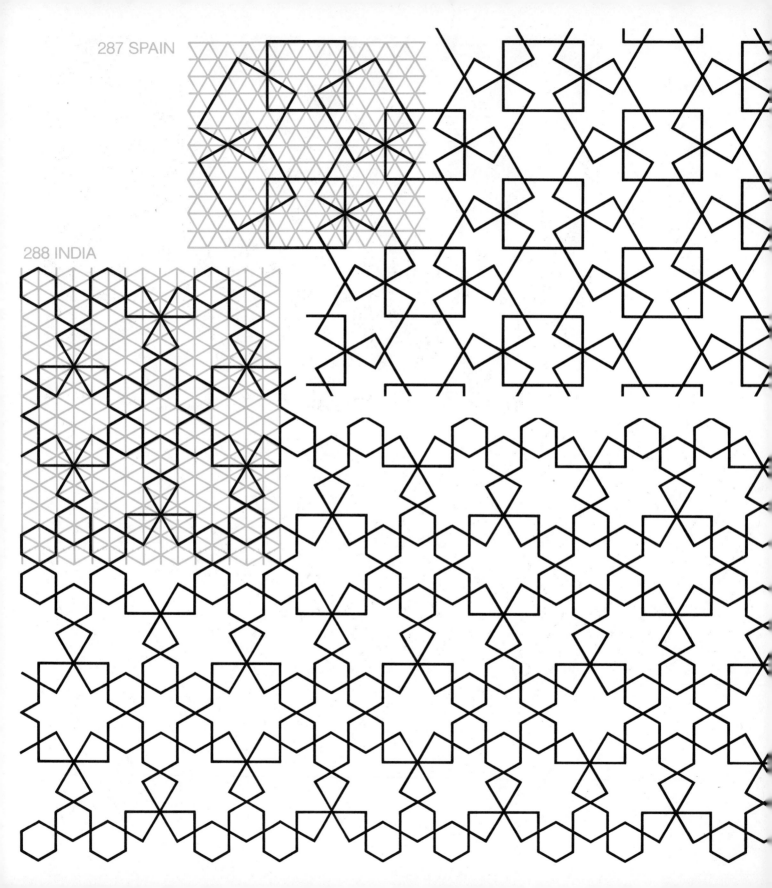

287 SPAIN

288 INDIA

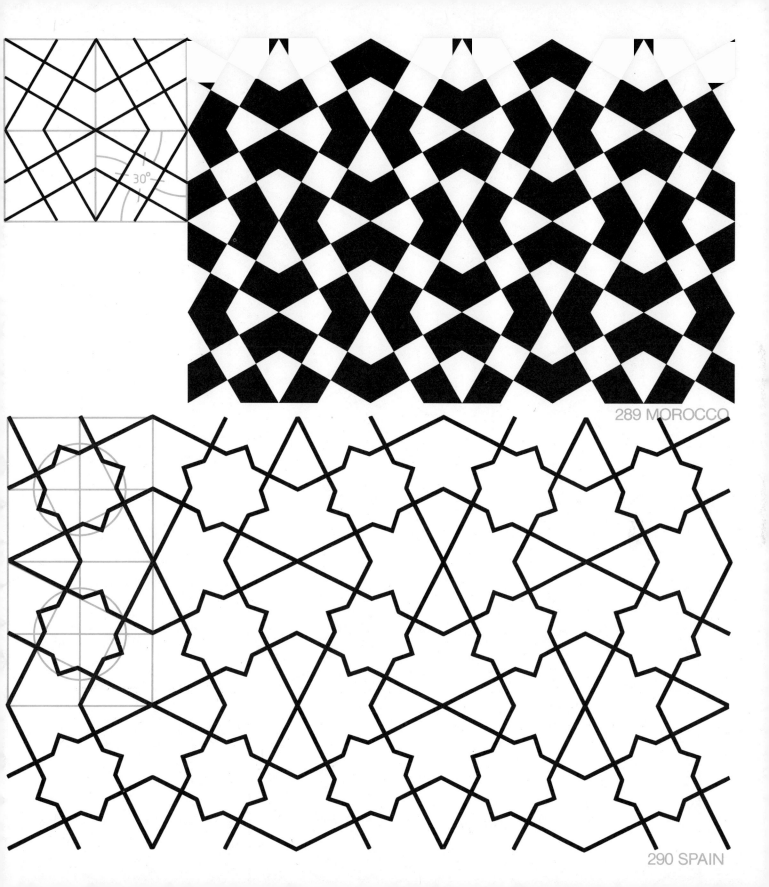

289 MOROCCO

290 SPAIN

293 EGYPT

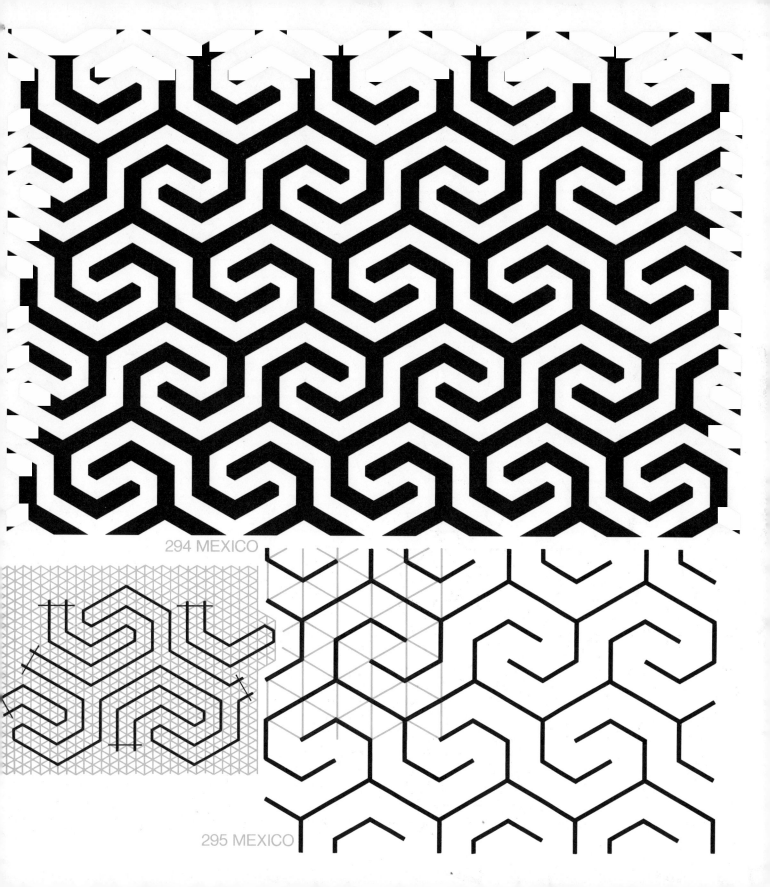

294 MEXICO

295 MEXICO

296 INDIA

297 IRAN

298 INDIA

299 EGYPT

300 SPAIN

301 SPAIN

302 TURKEY

303

304

305 IRAN

306 EGYPT

307 INDIA

308 IRAN (ref. 332)

309 SPAIN

310 INDIA

311 TURKEY

312 AFGHANISTAN

313 IRAN

314 TURKEY

315 EGYPT

316 SPAIN

317 IRAN

318 IRAN

319 IRAN

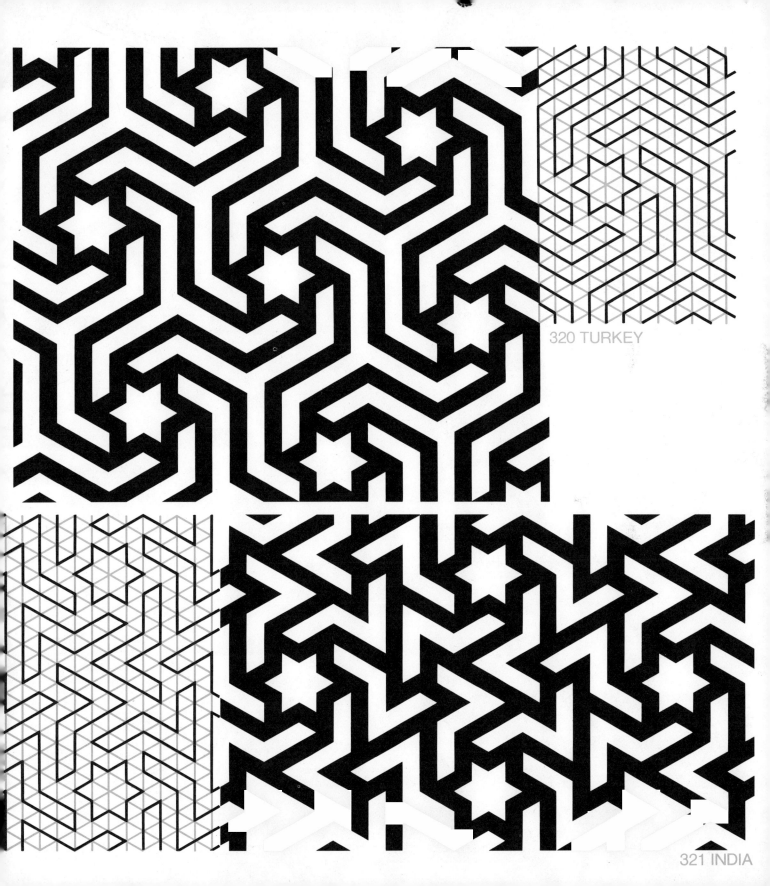

320 TURKEY

321 INDIA

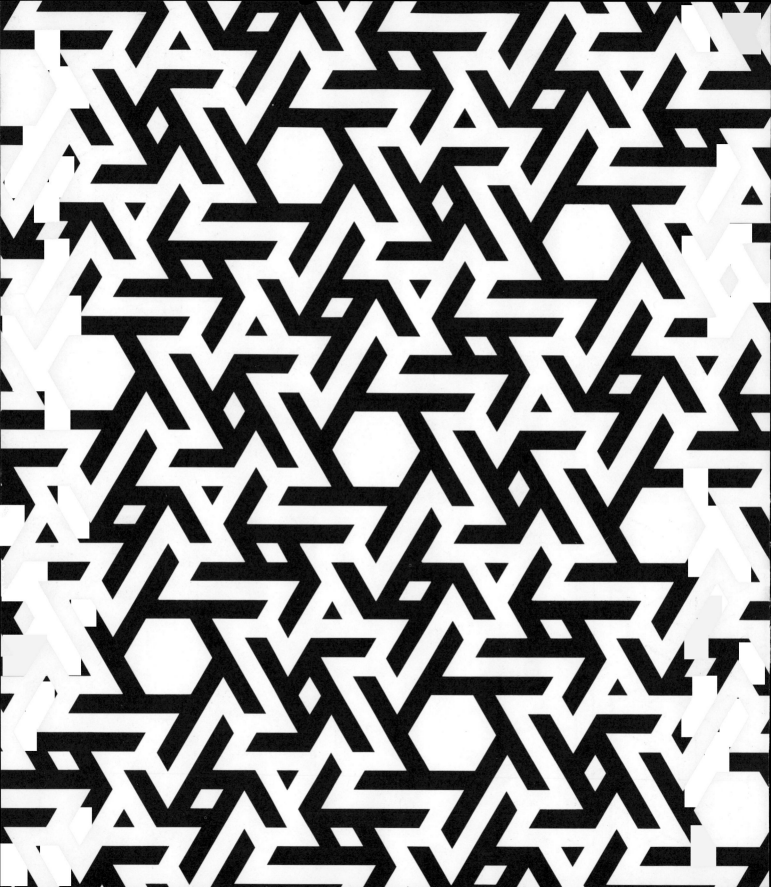

322 TURKEY

323 IRAN

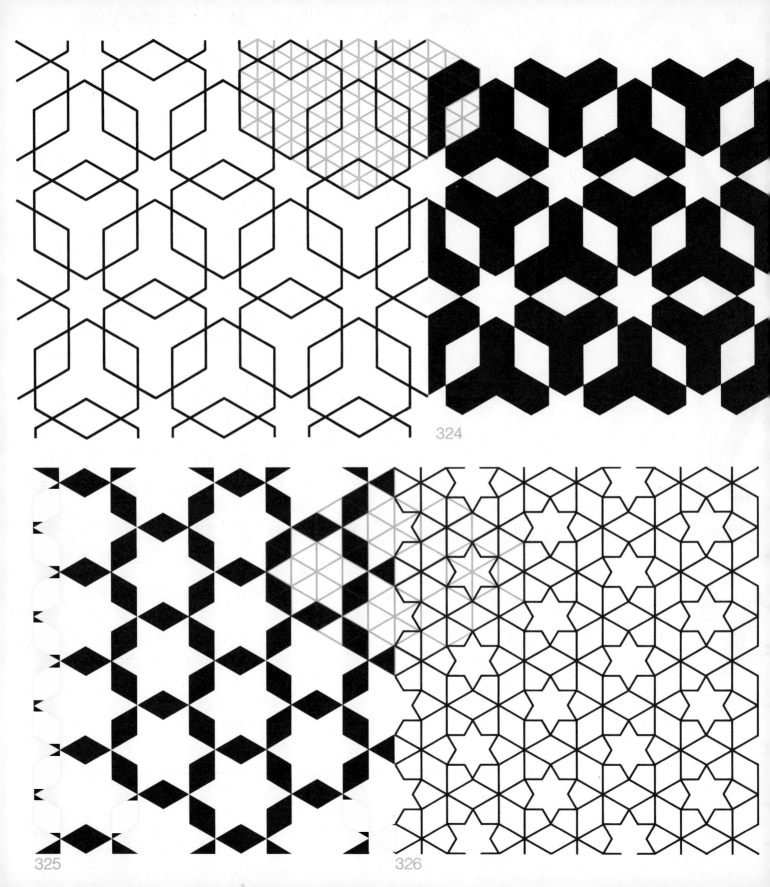

324

325

326

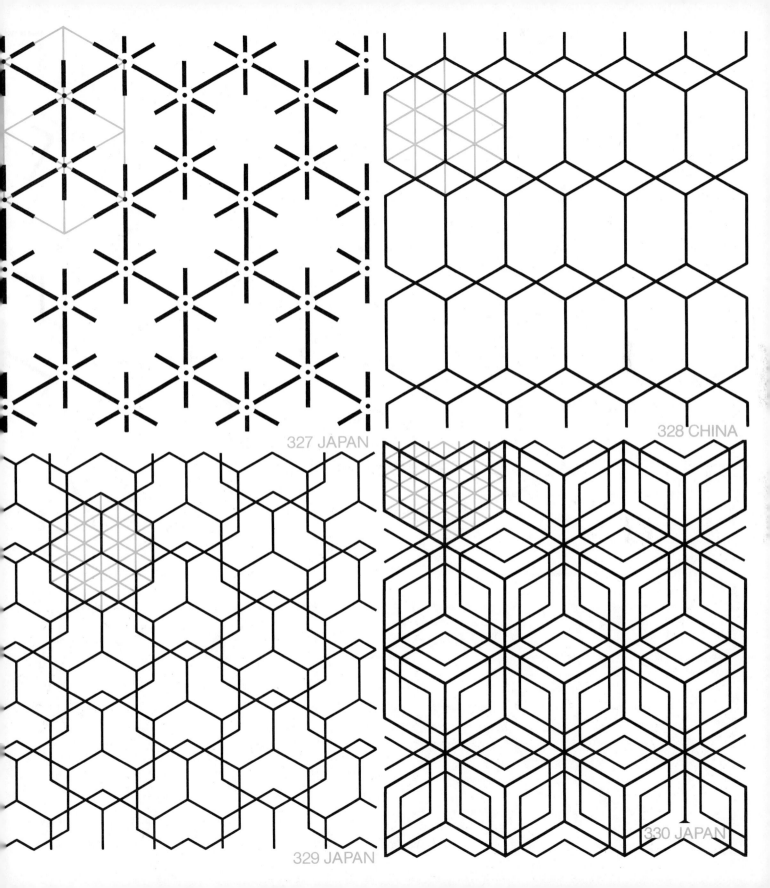

327 JAPAN

328 CHINA

329 JAPAN

330 JAPAN

331 IRAN

332 TURKEY

333 INDIA

334 CHINA

335 CHINA

336 CHINA

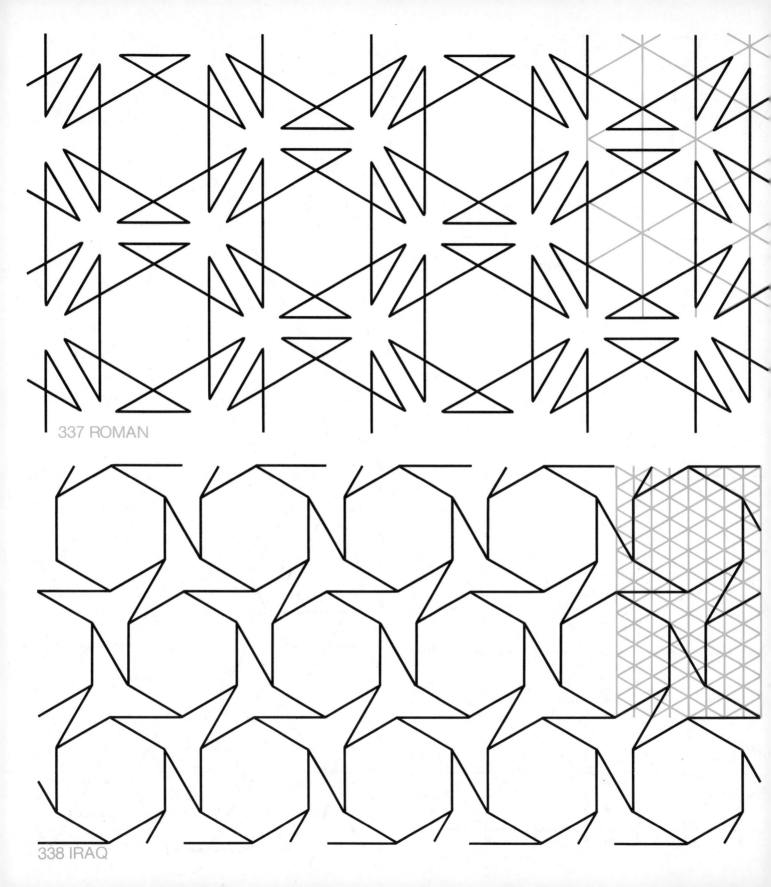

337 ROMAN

338 IRAQ

339 CHINA

340 CONGO

341 JAPAN

342

343

344

345

346 MOROCCO

347 SPAIN

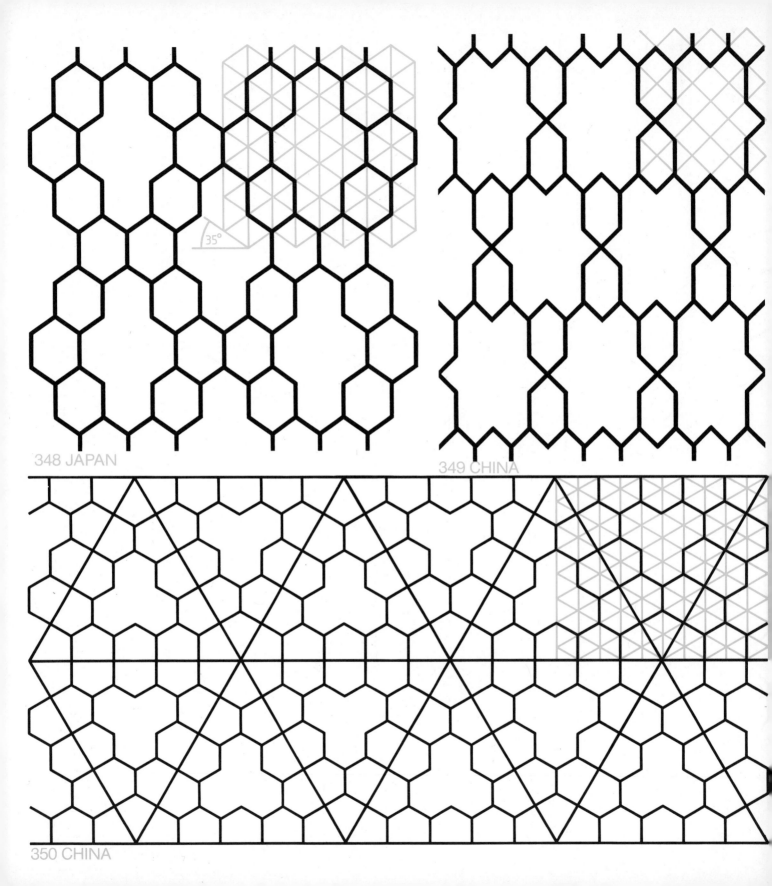

348 JAPAN

349 CHINA

350 CHINA

351

352

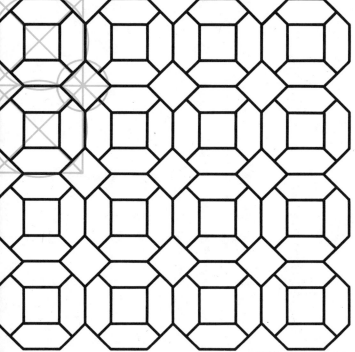

353 ROMAN

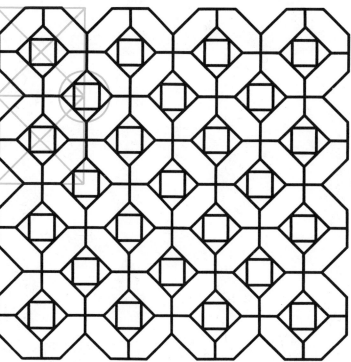

354 ROMAN

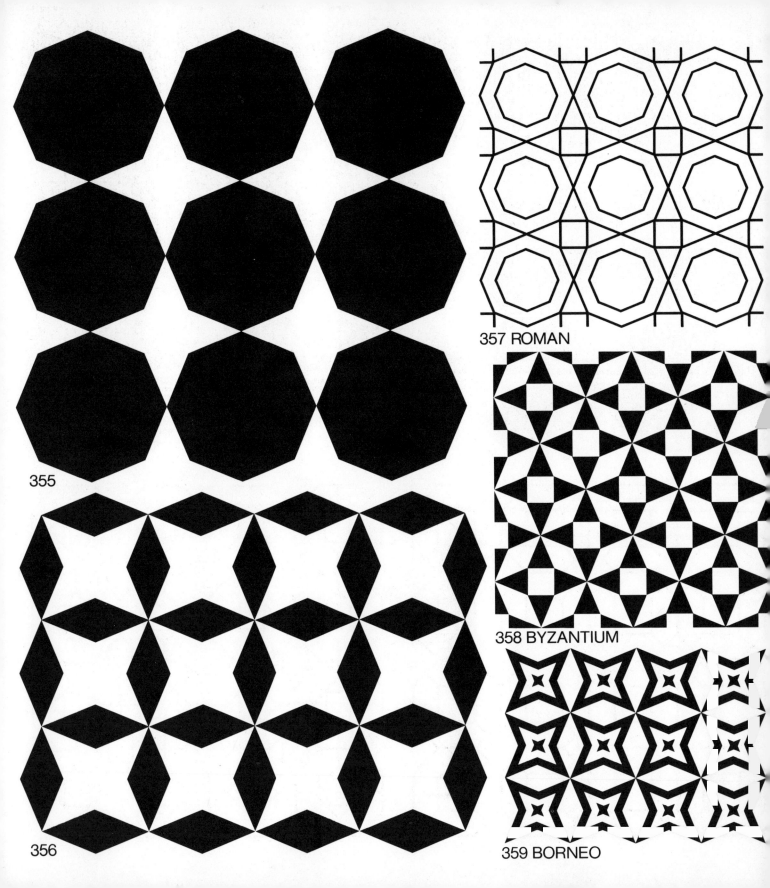

355

356

357 ROMAN

358 BYZANTIUM

359 BORNEO

360 MOROCCO

361 ROMAN

362 SPAIN

363 RUSSIA

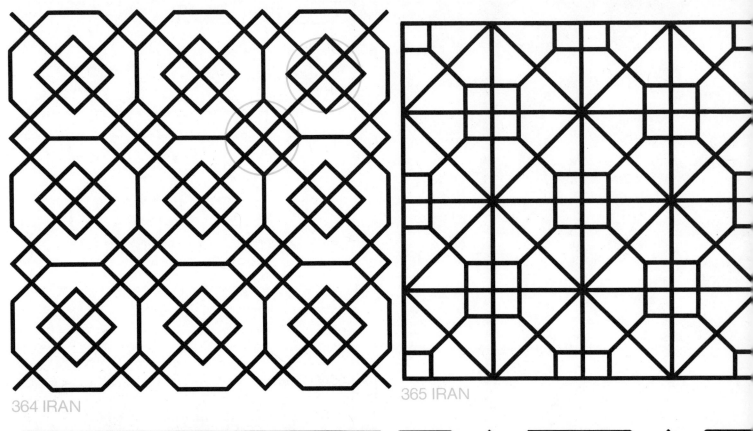

364 IRAN

365 IRAN

366 CHINA

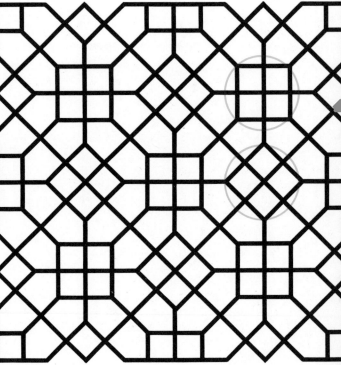

367 CHINA

368 SPAIN

369 BORNEO

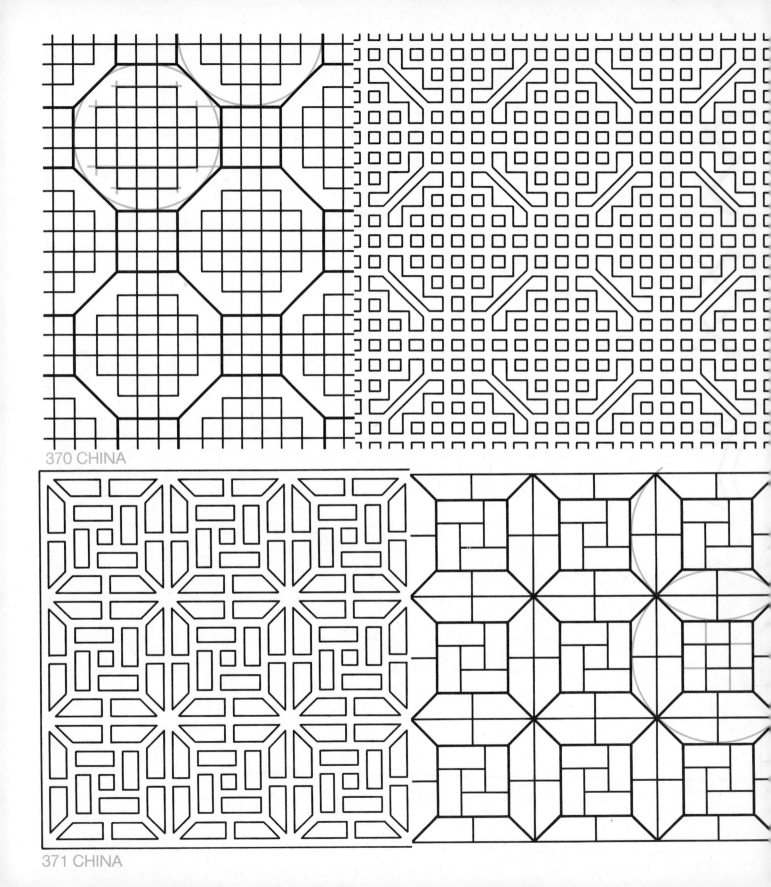

370 CHINA

371 CHINA

22.5°

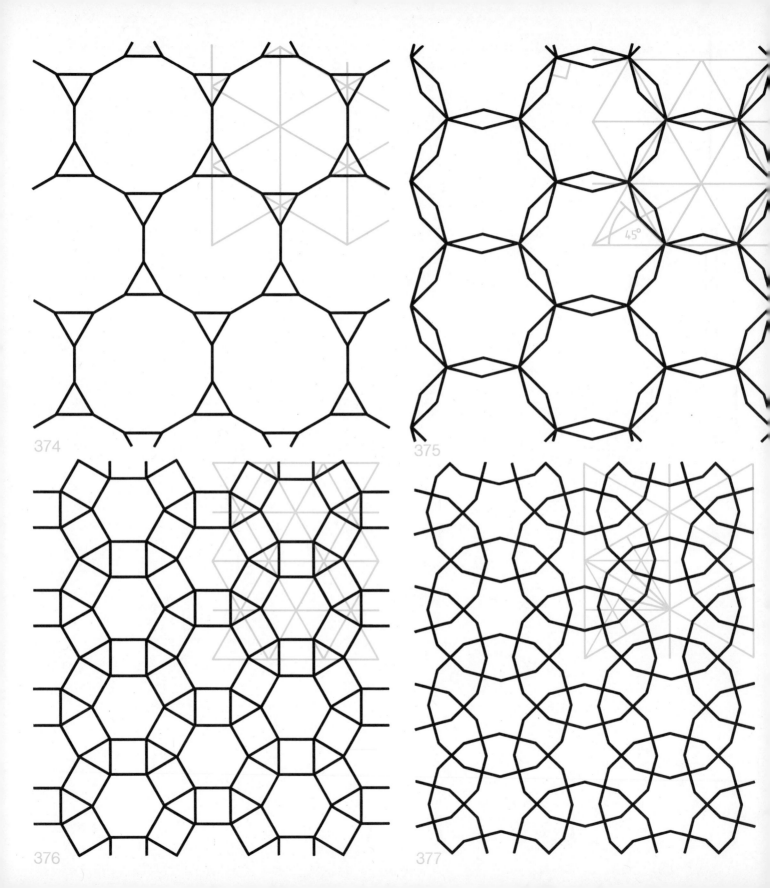

374

375

376

377

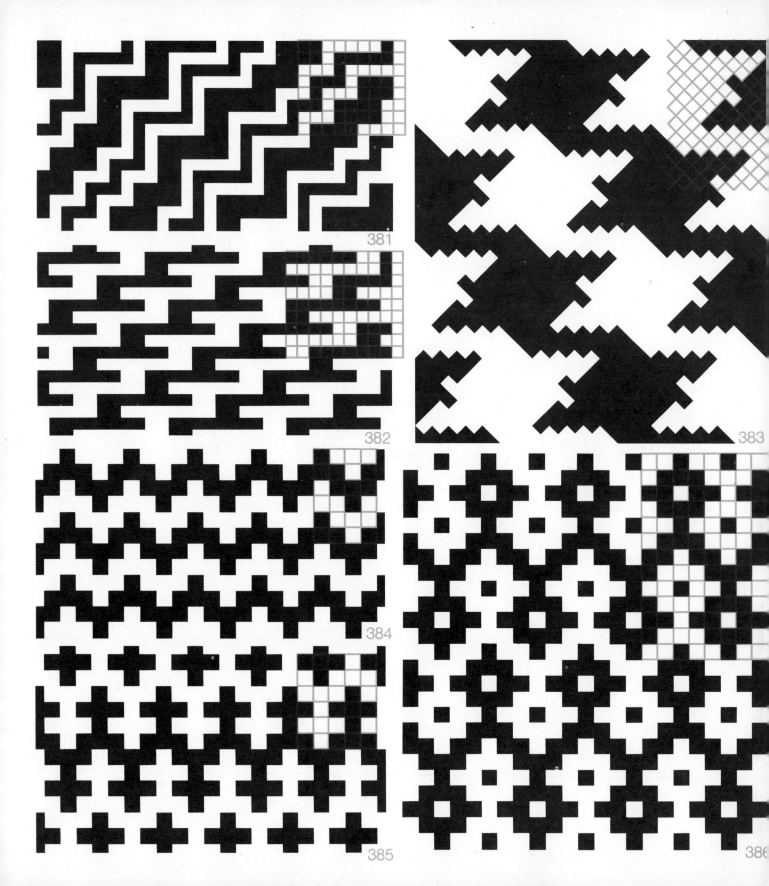

381

382

383

384

385

386

387 SPAIN

388 IRAN

389 EGYPT

390 ZAIRE

391 EGYPT

392 EGYPT

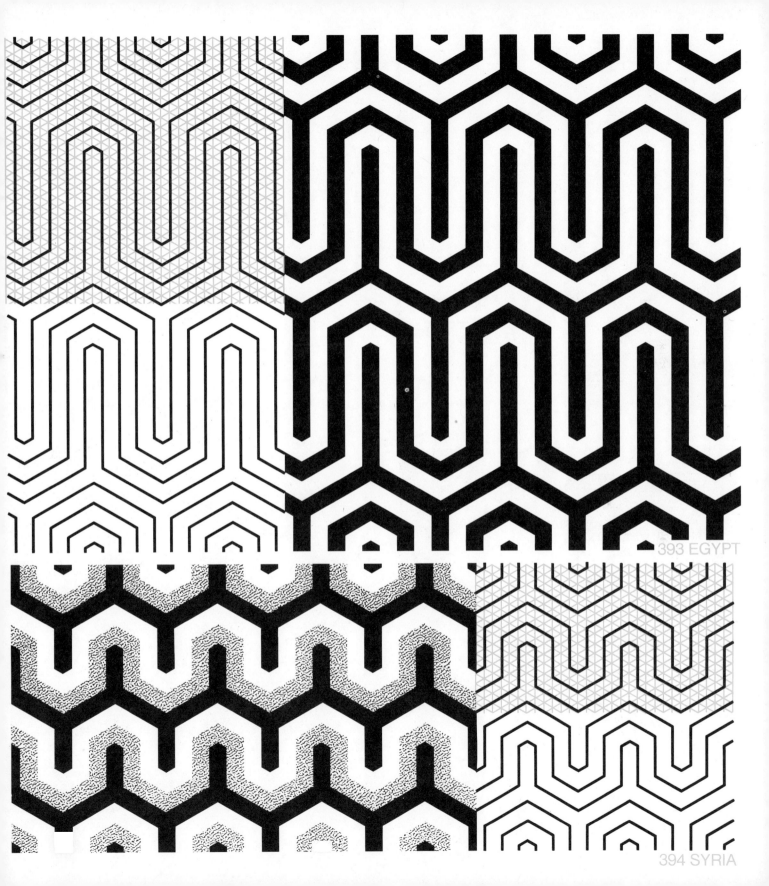

393 EGYPT

394 SYRIA

395 MOROCCO

396 ENGLAND

397 ENGLAND

398 JAPAN

399 IRAN

400 EGYPT

401

402 SPAIN

403 TURKEY

404 SPAIN

405 MOROCCO

406

407 IRAN

408 BUKHARA

409 AFGHANISTAN

413 MOROCCO

412 MOROCCO

416

417

418 INDIA

419 FRANCE

420 ITALY

421 ENGLAND

422 ENGLAND

423 CHINA

424 MOROCCO

425 IRAN

426 SPAIN

427 SPAIN

428 SPAIN

429 SPAIN

430 SPAIN

431 SPAIN

432 SPAIN

433 SPAIN

434 MOROCCO ↑   435 SPAIN ↓

436 SPAIN

437 SPAIN

438 SPAIN

439

440

441

442

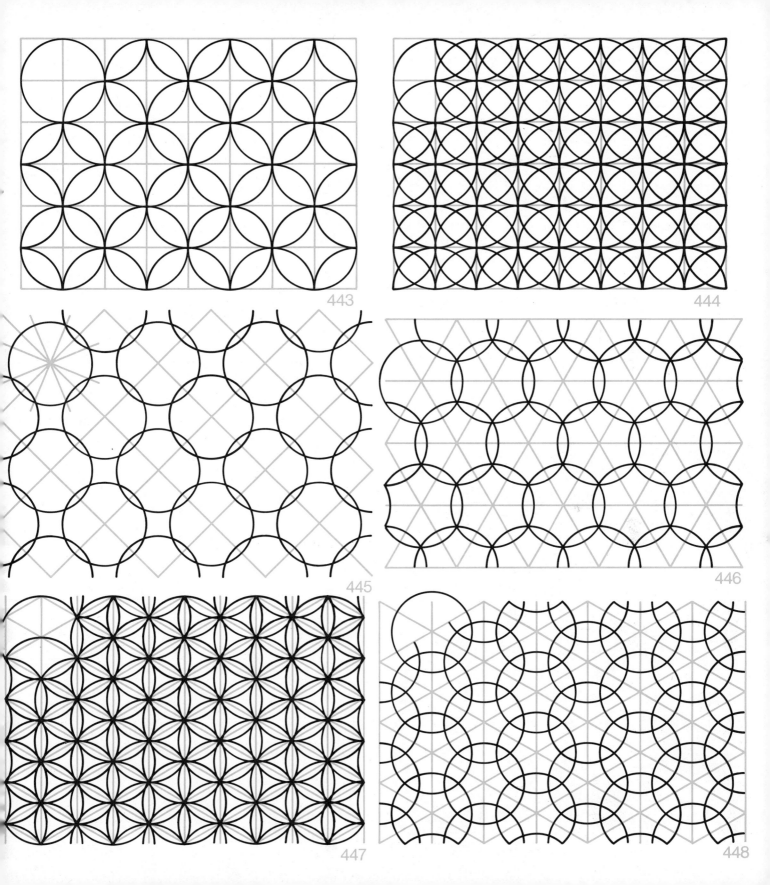

443

444

445

446

447

448

449 (var. 443)

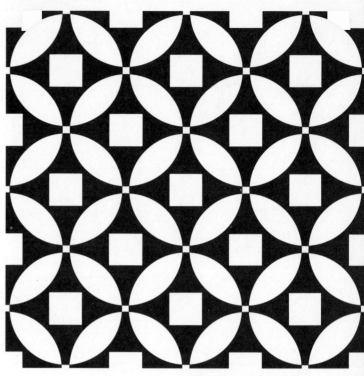

450 BYZANTIUM (var. 443)

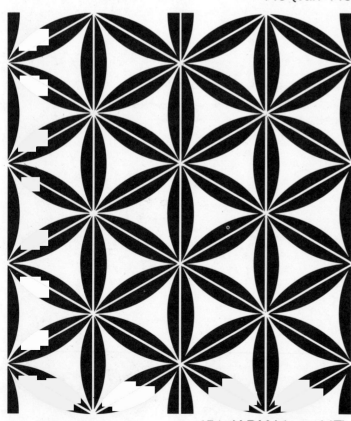

451 JAPAN (var. 447)

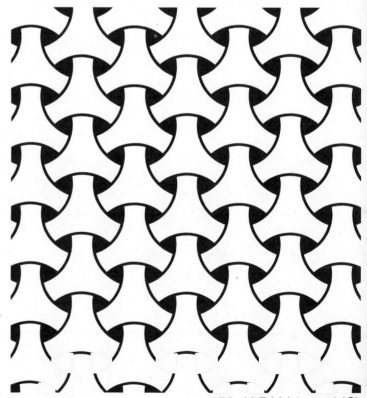

452 JAPAN (var. 448)

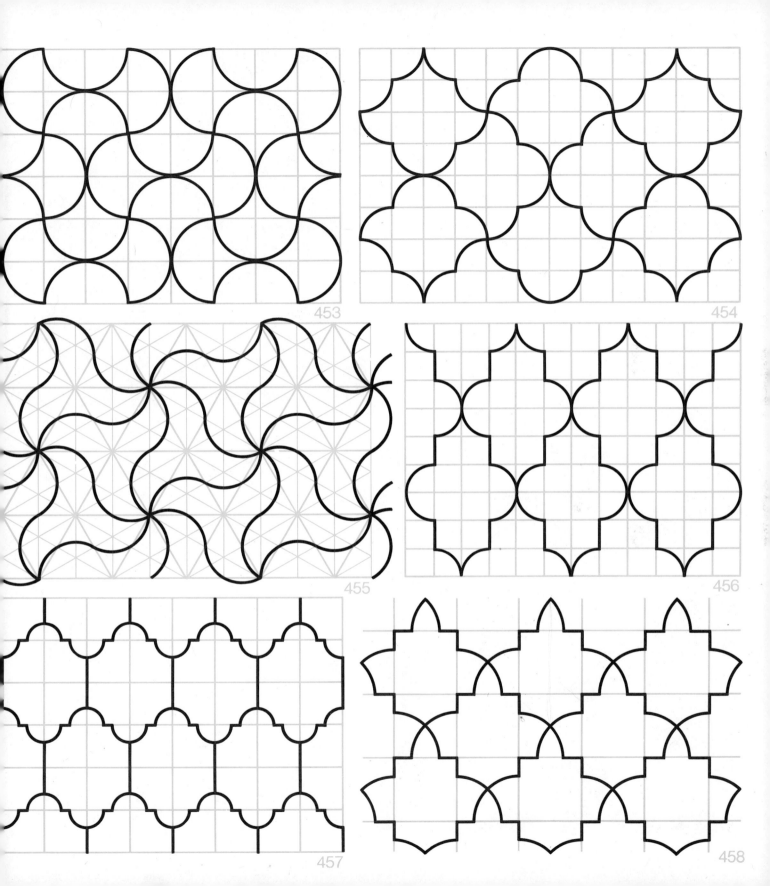

453

454

455

456

457

458

459 ITALY (var. 453)

460 INDIA (var. 454)

461 SPAIN (var. 455)

462 INDIA (var. 456)

58°

463 SPAIN (var. 458)

464 MOROCCO

465 GOTHIC (var. 445)

466 GOTHIC

467 ROMAN (var. 444)

468 WIDESPREAD ISLAMIC & BYZANTINE (var. 448)

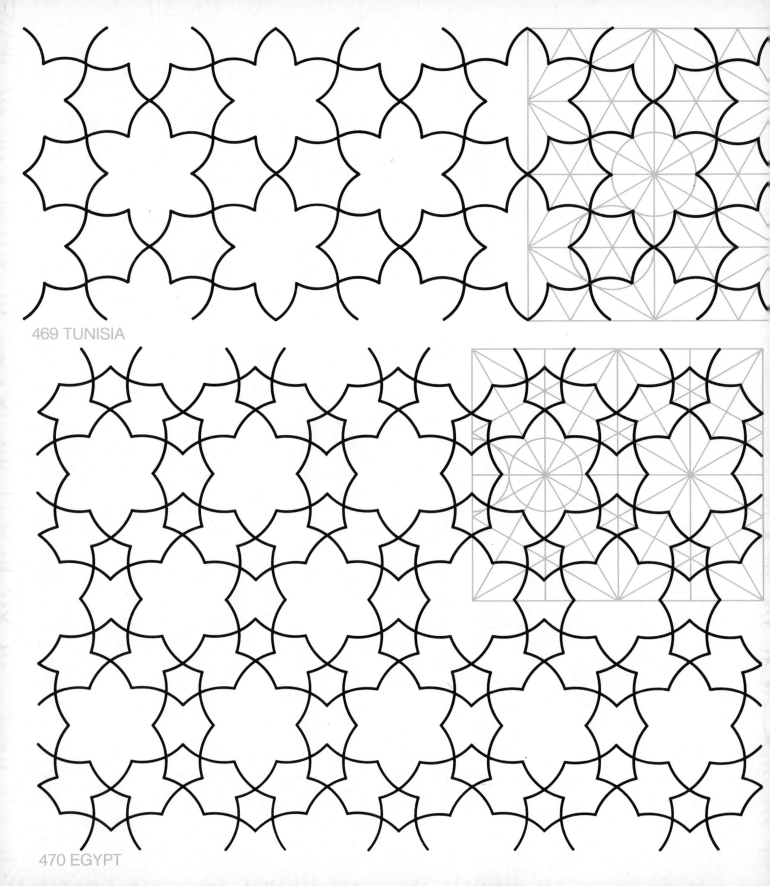

469 TUNISIA

470 EGYPT

471 SYRIA

472 SYRIA

473 SPAIN

474

475

476

477 CHINA

478 CHINA

479 BORNEO

480 BORNEO

482 BORNEO

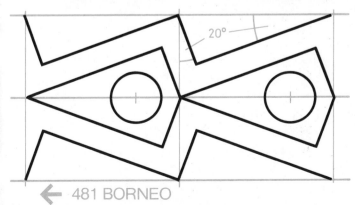

20°

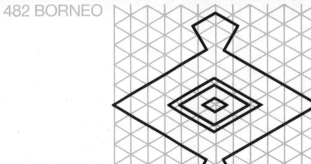

← 481 BORNEO

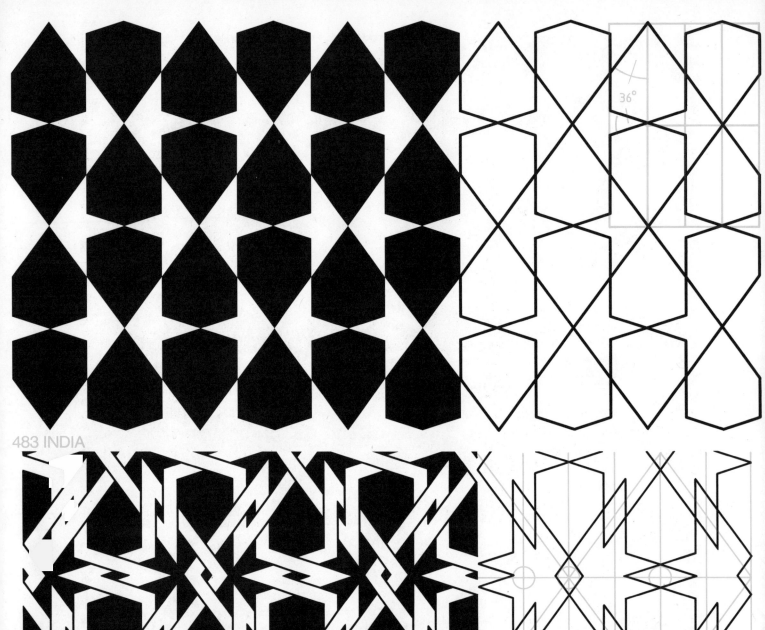

483 INDIA

36°

484 SPAIN (var. 483)

485 EGYPT

486 SPAIN (var. 485)

488

489

490

491

492

493

494

495

496

497

498 GREECE

499 GREECE

500 GREECE

501

502

503

504

505

506

507 MEXICO

508 SPAIN

509 IRAN

510 TURKEY

511 ECUADOR

512 CHINA

513 CHINA

514 CHINA

515 PERU

516 MEXICO

517 CELTIC

518 CELTIC

519 CELTIC

520 CHINA

521 MEXICO

522 MEXICO

523 YEMEN

524 YEMEN

525 YEMEN

526

527

528

529

530

531

532 MEXICO

533 CHINA

534 EGYPT

535 CELTIC

536 GOTHIC (ref. 387-390)

537 GOTHIC

538 GOTHIC

539 GOTHIC

540 EGYPT

541 EGYPT

542 EGYPT

543 TURKEY

544 EGYPT

545 EGYPT

546 CHILE

547 CHILE

548 MEXICO

549 CELTIC

550 CELTIC

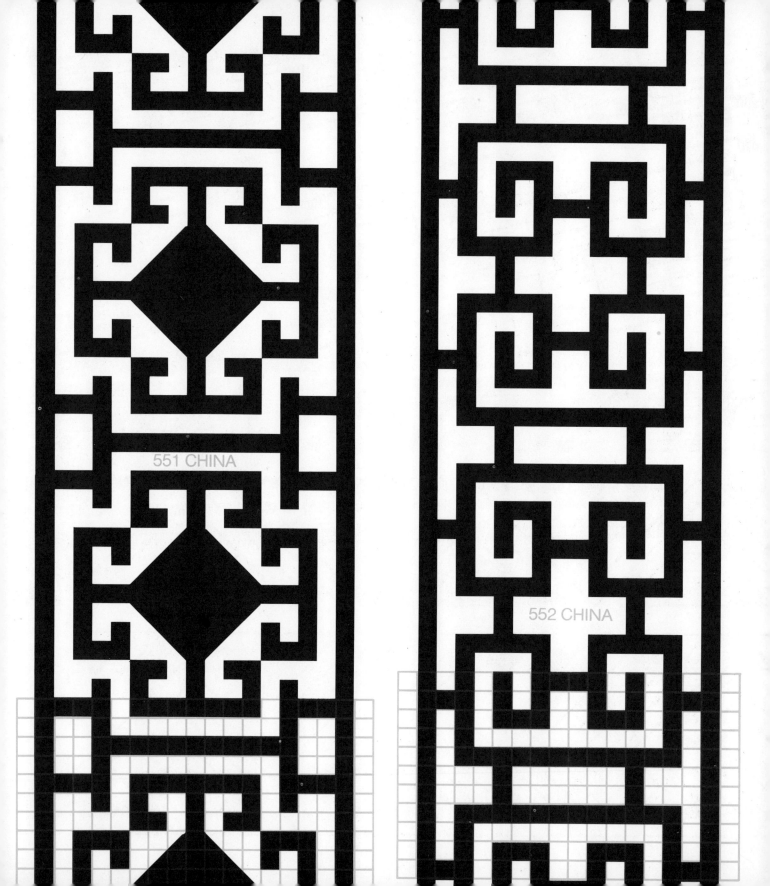

551 CHINA

552 CHINA

553

554

555

556 IRAN

557 IRAN

558 GOTHIC

559 MOROCCO

560 MOROCCO

561 SPAIN

562 NTH. AMERICAN INDIAN

563 NTH. AMERICAN INDIAN

564 PERU

565 MEXICO

566 GOTHIC

567 GOTHIC

568 FRANCE

569 TURKEY

570 TURKEY

22·5°

571 MEXICO

572 GOTHIC

573 EGYPT

574 GOTHIC

575 INDONESIA

576 EGYPT

577 CHINA

578 IRAN

579 TURKEY

580 GOTHIC

581 CHINA

582 CHINA

583

584

585

586 INDIA

587 INDIA

588 INDIA

589 INDIA

590 INDIA

591 SPAIN

592 TURKEY

593 GOTHIC

594 CELTIC

595 CELTIC

596 GOTHIC

597 ROMANESQUE

598 GREECE

599 ROMAN

600 GREECE